Jayneen Sanders

AWE

A little word for a big feeling

illustrated by
Camila Carrossine

Dear Parents, Caregivers and Educators

Research tells us that feelings of awe contribute to more positive mental health, make us more empathetic and less entitled, alter how we experience time by allowing us to savor moments and be more present, encourage curiosity and critical-thinking skills, lessen materialism, make us more generous and cooperative, and help us to connect to others and understand that the world is much bigger than us, and elevates our joy in being part of it. Awe seems to be a universal – peoples from all cultures report feeling this emotion. Helping your child to recognize feelings of awe can only be beneficial, as they embark on life's journey.

As you read this book with your child, take the time to talk about the illustrations and the concepts within, and encourage them to contribute by expressing their own experiences of awe and the feelings and sensations associated with it.

"In awe we understand we are part of many things that are much larger than the self."

Dacher Keltner from his book 'Awe: The New Science of Everyday Wonder and How It Can Transform Your Life'.

For Loren and Evie who inspired me to create this book. J.S.

Awe
Educate2Empower Publishing an imprint of
UpLoad Publishing Pty Ltd
Victoria Australia
www.upload.com.au

First published in 2025
Text copyright © Jayneen Sanders 2025
Illustration copyright © UpLoad Publishing Pty Ltd 2025

Written by Jayneen Sanders
Illustrations by Camila Carrossine

Jayneen Sanders asserts her right to be identified as the author of this work.
Camila Carrossine asserts her right to be identified as the illustrator of this work.

Designed by Astred Hicks

ISBN: 9781761160523 (hbk) 9781761160516 (pbk)

Dear Reader

"Awe is a little word for a big feeling. A feeling so big and spectacular that no words seem to come close to the feeling of awe. Awe fills me up from the tip of my toes to the top of my head. Awe brings me so much joy and I am always grateful."

Love Jayneen xx

**Before you turn the page,
I'd like you to do one small thing.**

On a warm clear evening or a cold cloudless night, lie on a blanket outside. Best to be away from bright lights and have a safe adult with you. Place a pillow under your head and stare up at the stars.

Keep staring while you silently count to 100.

Stay as long as you like.
The longer you stay, the more you will see.

Now turn the page.

What did you notice as
you lay under the stars?

How did you feel?

If you felt joy, if you felt wonder, if
you felt tingles or a heart so full …
that feeling is called

AWE.

AWE

is a little word
for a big feeling.

Whenever I look at the billions of stars on a clear night or see a big full moon change from orange to white as it climbs into the sky, my feelings of

AWE

are so big, I have no words.

I can only be in that moment
and feel that feeling.

AWE can be found in many places.
In small places like a garden
or in big places like the forest
or the ocean.

You can find AWE all around you when you stop, take the time and notice.

Some people look at a piece of
art and get that joyful, full-heart
feeling of AWE.

Some people swim in the ocean and as the cool crisp water runs over their body, they too have that feeling.

I'm older now. But when I was a little
girl, I lived on a farm. I rode my horse
Billy Mac nearly every day.

Billy Mac and my dog, Four Eyes,
were my best friends.

On warm summery days, we would ride down a grassy track near my house. I would tie Billy Mac up to the fence and Four Eyes and I would lie in the grass. While Four Eyes slept in the sun beside me, I would stare up at the bright blue sky. White fluffy clouds would drift by in all kinds of shapes. Sometimes I would close my eyes and feel the sun on my face. A feeling of joy and a heart so full would surround me like a cozy blanket.

A feeling of
AWE.

When have you felt
AWE?

Was it in a tall rainforest or
swimming in a rock pool?

Maybe climbing a mountain or
listening to a beautiful song?

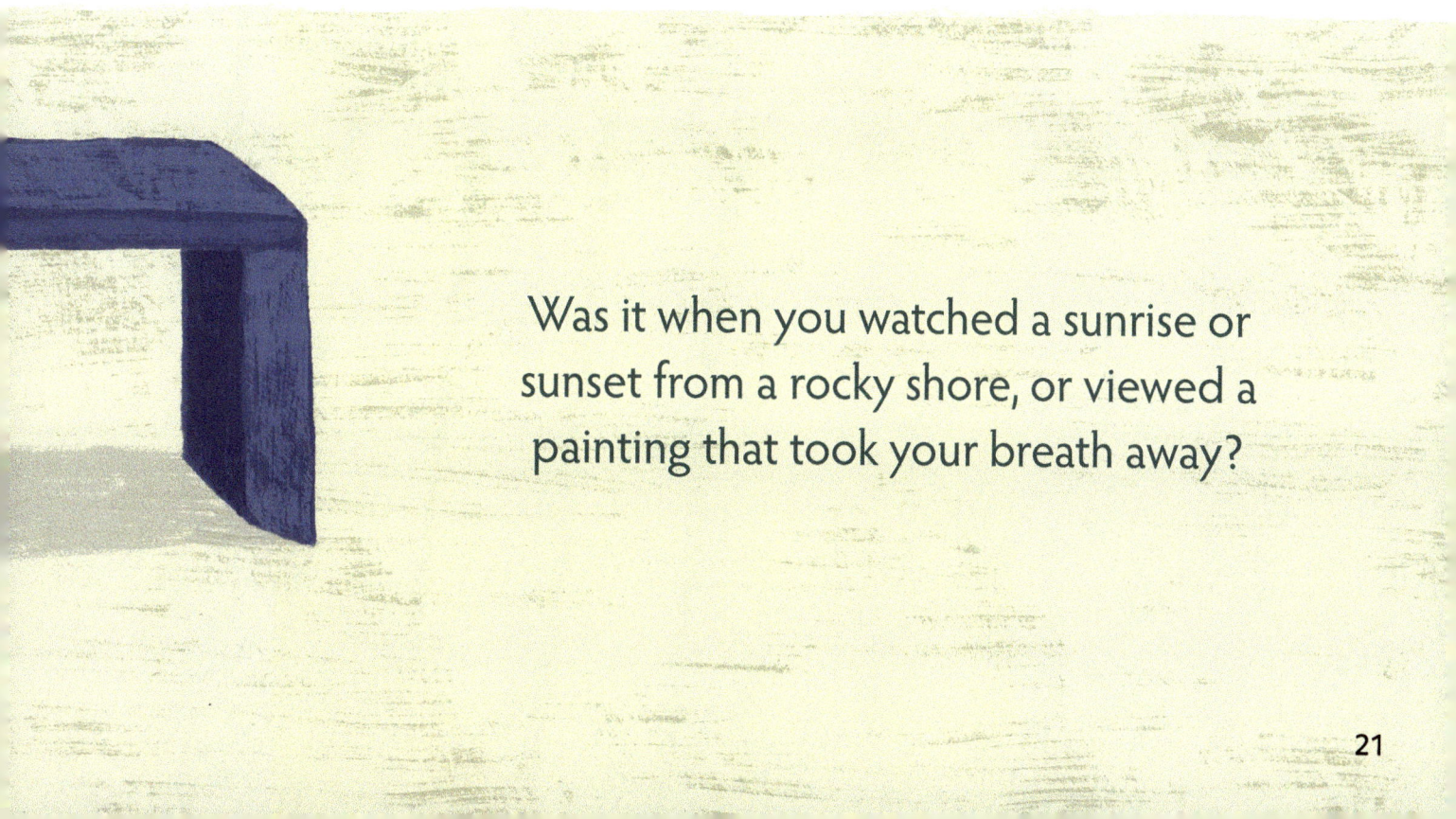

Was it when you watched a sunrise or sunset from a rocky shore, or viewed a painting that took your breath away?

Maybe it was something so
delicious that you will remember
the taste forever?

Or was it the smell of jasmine in early spring or the feeling of being loved?

AWE is all around us if we take the time to notice. You don't have to be on the top of a snow-covered mountain or parachuting out of a plane. It might simply be that you stopped. You looked, and you marveled at the perfect raindrop circles spiraling, one after the other, on a blue-green pond.

Maybe the smallest things can give
us the biggest feelings.

AWE gives us joy.
It gives us hope.
It fills our hearts
with wonder.

Find AWE in the saddest of times
and the happiest of times.

You don't have to search for AWE.

AWE is all around you.

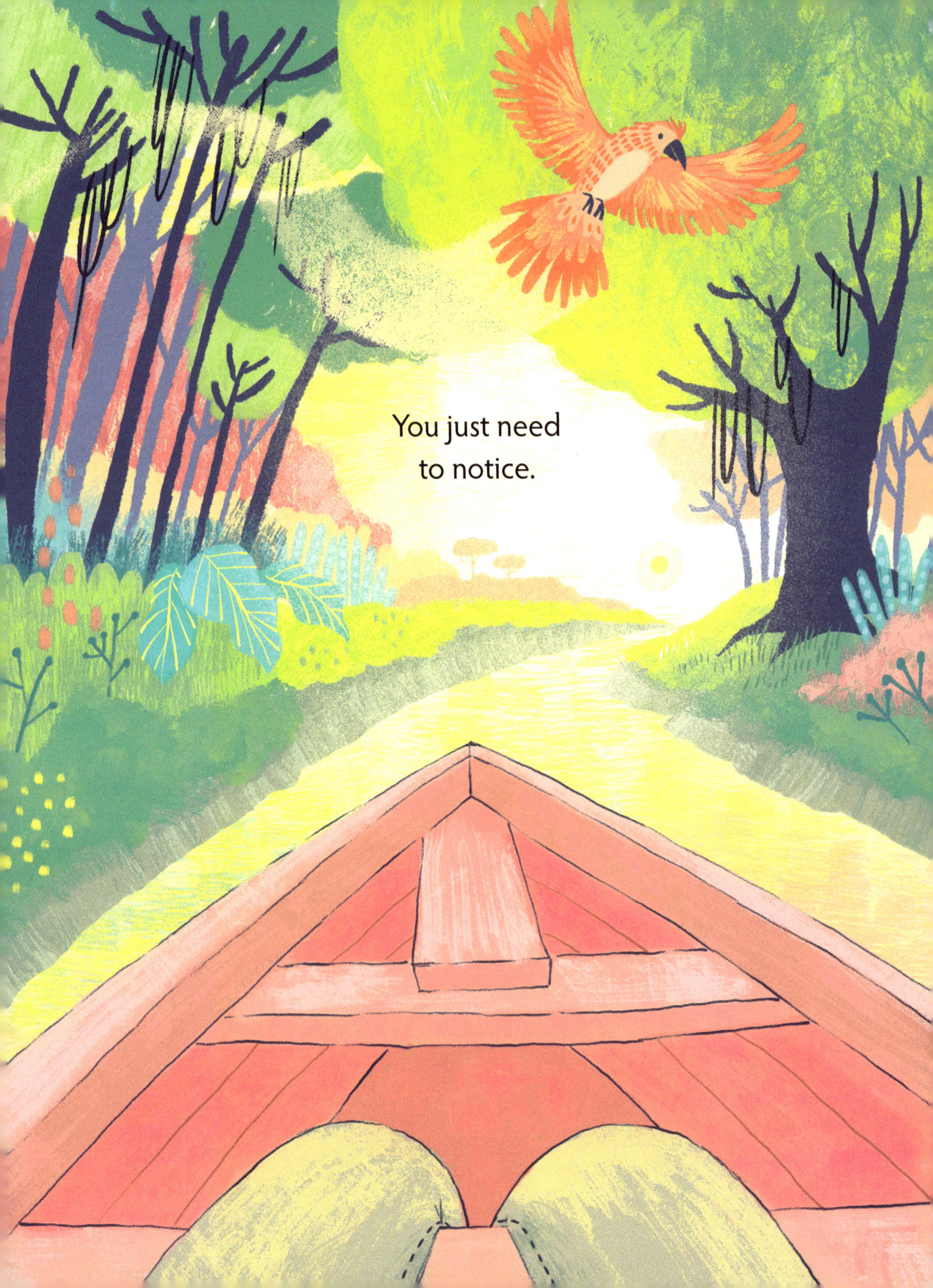

You just need
to notice.

www.ingramcontent.com/pod-product-compliance
Lightning Source LLC
Chambersburg PA
CBHW041636040426
42448CB00023B/3497